Getting Ready to Travel

poems by

Llewellyn McKernan

Finishing Line Press
Georgetown, Kentucky

Getting Ready to Travel

Copyright © 2017 by Llewellyn McKernan
ISBN 978-1-63534-119-5 First Edition
All rights reserved under International and Pan-American Copyright Conventions.
No part of this book may be reproduced in any manner whatsoever without written permission from the publisher, except in the case of brief quotations embodied in critical articles and reviews.

ACKNOWLEDGMENTS

"Vision." *Florida State Poets Association Annual Anthology* #33
"A Leaf Stiffens." *The Sow's Ear Poetry Review*
"Dog Monday." *Tantra*

Publisher: Leah Maines

Editor: Christen Kincaid

Cover Art: Original Pastel by Judith A. Lawrence

Author Photo: Johnson Photographic Studio

Cover Design: Elizabeth Maines

Printed in the USA on acid-free paper.
Order online: www.finishinglinepress.com
        also available on amazon.com

Author inquiries and mail orders:
Finishing Line Press
P. O. Box 1626
Georgetown, Kentucky 40324
U. S. A.

Table of Contents

I Wash the Dishes 1
Everything Suggests 3
This is Sunshine Hill 4
In Puddles 5
I Walk By a Church 6
Mozart's Great Mass 7
So Praise the Round Peg 8
I Dream New Dreams 10
If You're Wild and Willful 11
Now That I'm Old 12
Carol, Cry 13
Gray Bird 14
Dog Monday 15
She Loves the Mountain 16
The Angel 18
A Leaf Stiffens 19
The Toe of Her Shoe 20
I Make the Beds 22
I know Jack the Ripper 23
This Angel 24
When I Sleep 26
She's the Puppet 28
I Wake 30
I Shop for Today 31
Can You Draw 32
Vision 33

for Ashley, Kyle, and Alyssa
May God Bless All Your Travels

1

    I wash the dishes
watch the clock
Each tick is the echo of all I've lost

    I strip my lashes
of the sticky woes
I treated like friends fought like foes

    and set out
from this God-forsaken place
to find some remnant of the human race

All I've got
is a threadbare song
but it wraps me in furs when I'm cold and alone

    leaves me a silence
that just gets better when
it takes all my thoughts and puts them together

    all but the nightmare
of being in school
where I've lost my schedule I'm in the wrong room

    the exam's in French
the questions are ghouls
with the same awful answer: "You're a FOOL FOOL FOOL

    in front of the teachers
the students the chairs"
I crawl on the ceiling I stop breathing air. . . .

    "It's time" a voice calls And so
I awake Sweat-drenched, gut-
wrenched, and in a daze

    but aware at last Death can't
keep me here where my heart
gets smaller and

    smaller each year So I leave with
nothing I bravely walk
out of the circle

    I drew with my chalk

Everything suggests
            something it's not.
    Systems unravel and then
reknot.

            Waiting in Room 1-2-0
    is the line where I wait
    for *Waiting for Godot.*

    A mile-high windstorm,
            spinning with luck,
    lights on a flower, then it's nip
and tuck.

    My Chinese grandmother
with nothing to wear
        scrubs the stairs to the attic
        where she eats a pear.

    This barely done poem
I'll call my soul.
        It was new today
        before it got old.

　　　　This is Sunshine Hill
　　　　where I sit
　　　　　　for a spell. I ponder
　　　　sundogs, the smell
　　　　　　of a leaf, over-ripe
　　apples, the bitter
　　　　　and the sweet.

　　　　　I reflect on crime.
　　　　　　I examine dirt.
　　　　　　　　I take off my laminated
　　　　　lemon-colored skirt.
　　　　　　　　I take off my blouse,
　　my shoes and their laces.
　　　　　I watch

　　　　the sky swim
　　　　　and measure the graces
　　　　　　of countless great women
　　　that come
　　and go.

　　　　　They dance with joy.
　　　　　　I know what I know.

4

In puddles where all the dirt's been banished,
trees step backward until they vanish.

The Stairs of Heaven are paved with gravel
like the hours of the day where we all travel.

An earthly hound sniffs with his nose.
The Hound of Heaven goes where he goes.

The poor in spirit string prayers together
like links on a chain lighter than a feather.

All things shatter, become what is.
Unshakable solids turn to fizz.

The Daughter of God is the Daughter of Man.
She does very little, but she does what she can.

5

      I walk by a church
   and turn my head.
      I walk by a creek, my soul is lead:

   I lose myself
      in the center of an hour that
slowly expands like the bud of a flower.

      In the church choir
   an angel with hair
      the color of flame sits in my chair.

   Since I am absent,
      she sings my songs,
and plays the downbeat on bongo drums.

      God reveals to me
   that Little Brother Right
      works by day, reworks the night.

   And Big Sister Wrong,
      with blood on her sleeve,
is mother to the child we call Mystery.

    Mozart's great mass is incomplete,
   my compulsions keep playing,
      even in my sleep.

To walk around naked is really no sin.
 Honesty's
where fiction begins.
  The map of the psyche is
fretted with holes, a filter through which
God strains the soul.

    When you tune your piano,
leave one note flat.
Not knowing where you are is where you're at.

 Sand in the eyes, sand under stars,
   sand in December, sand on Mars—
the word's the same but each one recalls
   something not found
in the others at all.

    To tell you the truth, I once
saw a man
   with three shining crosses, one in each hand,
and one in his left eye, it burned like a fire
    where a thousand angels from a heavenly choir
    praised your toenails, my moon-round cheeks,
     the spell-bound lemmings that find what they seek.

Somewhere or other
on this finite globe
     an infinite dream is being swallowed whole.

7

   So
praise the round peg
  for squaring off
    for parallel bars of light and dark
     you see
at a distance
  or from a great height.
  Praise the colors in black that
  lead
to white.

  Praise
birds in pairs, birds
  in a flock
that take on a shape
(between ticks of a clock) fluid
   as your own blue-veined pulse
or the creek
that rises
and falls to dust.

  Praise
  the constant order that spins
on a dime, the egg
  that breaks open
just in time. Praise the place
in your heart where the power
that turns
water to ice, Keats

     to the urn, speaks softly
in silence
  the thunder of your name.
(Once that happens
  you won't be the same.)

Praise the moment in time
 that admits the eternal, and
 omnipotent God who
 lives, wholly human.

8

        I dream new dreams.
I get all stirred up. Can I eat with a spoon?
              Can I drink from a cup?

Deep kisses are work, but so is dread
  of tomorrow and suffering and dying
    in bed.

I like my steak raw
      if I don't see it bleed.
I'm torn by indifference. I'm torn by need.

      Bread for beggars
I knead with my thumbs. At times it cries out.
    More often it's dumb.

      All that is natural
        holds up the unseen.
          I'm sinking in quicksand
up to my knees.

9

If you're wild and willful, uncertain as me,
  If you beat your words bloodless,
disturb a still sea.
  If what you call joy is what you call pain,
and nothing is ever exactly the same,

              If you scream
when you're silent, scream when you talk,
                  rule on what's fair,
 but always find fault,

     If you walk on the living,
  live with the dead,
      make love to no one except in bed.
If thunder scares you, and lightning, too,
      and sitting down and putting on your shoes,

and walking toward any of your doors
      means you're going to lock it—read

no
more.

> Now that I'm old,
> I'm shy and unpopular.
> > So I fast and figure in The Ever After.

> I check to see if my slip
> is hanging
> > and if my hormones
> > are really changing.

I stare in the mirror to see if my blemish
> is real
or imagined from start to finish.
I'm baptized with flaws
in the perfect river.
> I take in the morgue
and its *mortis rigors*.

I list all my foes, they reach 70 times seven.
> I burn up what I love
in a too hot oven.
> > I'm a puppet on a string that goes sky-high.
> But nobody pulls it except when I lie.

> I repeat all I hear. I work my brain.
> Sometimes I think I'm going insane.

11

Carol, cry, curse, and screech,
       howl in the cold,
howl
in the heat.
        Bawl and beg, beseech and moan—
     as you lie on your largest
and smallest bone.
            Grieve and mourn, keen and complain
     when all you meet
don't know your name.
          Pule and rage, sob and squall
     for the all in one, and the one in all.

Wail
and whimper, snivel, whine
     shout and yelp, hoot and repine,
sough and weep, boohoo, exclaim,
     rage and roar, raise hell like Cain

       when his Father caught him
with blood on his hands, his eyes
 a grand slam
     with hate in them.

     The mark the boy got, stamped on his ear
     a deafening silence that he couldn't bear.

12

Gray bird sitting in my Sunday dream
Unwrap the silver from its one big scene

Red bird perched on my front porch steps
Eat all the crumbs my words have left

Blue bird flying to the chinaberry tree
Bring back the world before I was me

Black bird caught in the gold of my eye
Tell me no truths tell me no lies

White bird ruffling the center of the pond
Give me those circles before they are gone

Green bird opening the gate of the wind
Bring me the land where love never ends

Holy bird hovering at the edge of the sea
Lift up your wings as you dive toward me

Ghost bird feeding on Heaven's gold throne
Bring me back God's great thighbone

Fire bird burning the flesh of the beast
Eat every morsel until there is peace

13

Dog Monday hunted the prince of peace.
Cat Tuesday slept with a bowl of beef.

Bird Wednesday glued the world to a bone.
Fish Thursday whispered, "Leave me alone."

Bear Friday shaved the words to an ark.
Satyrday sang, "We're parts of a part."

Seal Sunday sat and knitted a sock
by the door that waited for someone to knock.

She loves the mountain she has to climb.
    Each step is a leg up, a joyous cry
from the straining muscles that strengthen her thighs.

    Each stone she walks on tells her it's wise.
Her soles grow tough, her sweat sublime.
    To have or have not is on the line.

On one side's a wood full of touch-me-nots
    where old men sleep with the bride of thoughts.
On the other's a desert, lightning-bright,

    full of instant replays just out of sight.
Snow freckles the sky with its dots and dash.
    Below it's sunny, and armies clash.

The blood in her wrist aches with vision.
    The marrow in her bone makes a decision.
She stretches her arms, her thumbs and fingers.

    The dead weight of her body rounds and lingers
on a crumbling cliff-hanger till a passionate air
    winds its reedy song about the roots of her hair,

and puffs of hot smoke from the guns below
    scorch her buttock—and—up she goes!
Breathless and briery, and buttery thin

    her body collapses to pearls and gems.
On this plateau everything moves
    to the stately rhythms of a rare perfume.

When she looks back, all she can find
        are prints in mud leading her to a mine
with a mouth small as the buzzing of a bee,

        telling her the truth about you and me.
A cedar ruffles its pale blue spokes.
        The clouds of the sky shine as they molt.

15

The angel that carries each soul in her lap,
The maple tree with bark-bringing sap,

all the words with meanings that lie,
all that dreams, and you and I

and the eggs in the hens the color of gold,
the barn in the meadow, the tales untold,

the Book of Wisdom, the sword with two sides
that slices all things into death and life,

the computers with discs, blank and free
as you in my arms, loving me, me, me—

are nothing but ashes in a cup of flame,
everyone is guilty, no one's to blame.

A leaf stiffens,
then it bends, and
  then it clings to the post of a fence.
    Next it floats
on the surface of a creek,
splitting fine hairs in a fit of pique.

   Now it springs
from the trap of the wind, lithe
  and lovely, liquid with fins,
    until it quarrels with the sap
in its veins (Both argue
      pretty much the same).

     So it turns red-gold, brown
and purple,
modeling itself on an old wood turtle.
   It digs in with claws,
and makes its own turf. It
     slowly builds a little egg of earth
       where it buries itself to
grow new life, vanishing like the others
     in the well of my eye.

17

        The toe of her shoe sprouts duct tape.
     She gets to her booth though it takes all day.
    Her sharp old face is delicately sprinkled
with tufts of hair and soap-opera wrinkles.
Her false teeth jiggle in a mouth full of gums.
  She once had a daughter.
   She once had a son.

       The speech of her hands is fine as an artist's.
      On one a ring sparkles like a spring in a forest.
     Her little blue hat has a row of pearls.
   She smiles, she chatters as if a real girl
sits opposite her and listens and nods.
  Is the old woman crazy
    or is she just odd?

       Who'll pay for this meal and leave a tip?
     The old woman chuckles and licks her lips,
    oiled by an omelet, a Double Deluxe with
   several secret grease-congealed crusts.
The words of her story fall, one by one.
  She once had a daughter.
   She once had a son.

       The stream of her words, rehearsed, unrehearsed,
     flows toward a darkness embraced by this verse.
    The name of the game begins with P: Penance
   and Prayer and Pain and Peace crack open
the hull of whatever's evil.
  "Just eat the vile thing.
   Don't cavil. Don't quibble."

    She winks her good eye. The other one is bad.
    The love she buried has risen, not glad but leavened
   by the best and the worst.
  She stands on short legs.
Fuzz clings to her skirt.
   Words spring from her lips with the power of a gun.
   She once had a daughter.
     She once had a son.

       She walks with stiff hips, she stumbles a little.
    Her life is quite plain, her life is a riddle.
What's left in her booth is a glass of tea
where the ice becomes what it used to be.
What more to be written on this small sheet?
  Life isn't short.
   Life isn't sweet.

18

I make the beds. I set the table
        for both the believer and the rebel.
        I boil the water I take from the creek.
I work by the day. I work by the week.

I fill the pantry. I empty the pail
        of whatever it is that I do so well.
        I salt the real with the absurd.
I store the unseen with what can't be heard.

Daylight and dark I break into crumbs
        that feed the birds, one by one.
        All the waste from babble and bile
I wash away, I wipe up with a towel.

I dust and mop, and shine and shower.
        What gleams for you I've polished
        for hours. This dull routine goes on and on.
Sometimes I like it but it's never fun.

I have the dirty job of making things clean.
Once that is done, they say what they mean.

19

I know Jack the Ripper and Jack Palance.
       I know Master Card, the King of Finance.
I know how laundry breaks up into two.
I know
how to get and hold the blues.

I know
that if lovers forget how to be
       naked as the moon swimming in the sea,
and babies in cribs forget how to rock,
and all that starts going
forgets how to stop,
       and my soul and my body
no longer speak,
and the pen I push no longer squeaks,
   and my words dry up in the middle
 of a phrase,
and this goes on
for days and days,
   and you, the axis on which my world turns
leaves me to shatter,

and I have to learn
that all I've strived for is sheer vanity—then
I don't know what
would become of me.

20

This angel
is a sweet young zebra-striped
        thing. Once it had scales.

Now it has wings.
        Its beak is bonny,
its breast is yellow. When it wants

to be heard,
it knows how to bellow.
        Feed it some shoestring, feed it

        some lace. Feed it
your flesh, tell it
  to its face how skinny

its neck is, how wrinkled
        its socks, how shabby the rug
where it sits and rocks.

A lover by night,
        a servant by day, it reminds
you of all

there is yet to say.
  When the moon comes out
and knocks down the door, when

all the stars
  have nothing to adore, this angel
is known

for its high-flown speech,
  for coming at once
when your blood needs a leech.

It will take your death
   in its tiny green claw and squeeze
it to death. But that's an old saw.

21

When I sleep
  on my side, the whole world
turns. When I sleep on my belly
I'm earth,
  gathering ferns. When I sleep
     on my back, I curl up my toes.
I dream my own dreams.
I breathe through my nose.
     I love

the little ghost that comes
  when I'm cold
and builds a red fire that
turns
          to gold
all that is wooden, little
by little,
  while I walk around
    playing the fiddle.

     When Midnight comes,
it's saintly as the dog
  wading in the stream
of the Very Odd. (If you
    model in clay, take it from
this brook. On its bank a tree grew

that now lives in a book—
  the pages its weather
  come home
to roost, letters budding
  and branching
    from a single shoot.)

      And when I can't sleep
for a year or two,
I mend
  all my fences,
  get rid of my suits.
I walk
  with the prayer that shapes
what's real. This cures

      my insomnia
and pays my bills.

      I put Werewolf to bed,
and the Vampire, too. Steam open
 forever what's
always been glued.
  Just

at the moment
I turn out the light,
      Big Shot and Big Bucks
come by for a bite.

22

                She's the puppet, but
   he's on a string in this story
of They
Have Everything.

   He wears his pants a little too tight.
She loves to be pinched,
                but not all night.
   He's the Ice Cream Emperor,
  all he knows
melts in the sun, freezes in the snow.

She's the Boogie-Woogie Witch.
       Her lips are wise
and really quite smooth, except for the places
              where they've been chewed.
       His legs are long and bowed and funny,
the hair on her head is soft as a bunny's.

   They live outdoors. They eat bear meat.
       The feather of her thigh
tickles his teeth.
       They wash in a basin the size of a nickel.
She calls him wise when he calls her fickle.
       They drink nut-brown
the juices of a swamp, plant
   pink roses in the middle of a romp,
blow down houses made of straw—
       Wolfman & Woman! View them with awe.

   They rinse out their wounds,
and tell them stories, and cheer up their scars
      by calling them gory.
Sometimes they wake
  in the middle of the night
    and watch the moon or start a fight.

    Then the stars come on
          in waves that move
the darkness to a place
              that they can love.

                    They drive forever
in a hot pink truck.
    God sticks out a thumb.
They pick Him up.

23

    I wake, full of crust
as a piece of bread. I kill the living,
resurrect the dead.

    My three great-aunts,
  dinosaur-old, sip tea in the parlor
with fingers of gold.

    My one great-uncle
  holds a trout on his line, heavy
as truth when it's hooked in time.

    God is too wide,
  this poem is too narrow, and faith
moves the world in its little wheelbarrow.

    Rain falls on the window
  like stars from heaven. Sun falls on your
face, a benediction. Water taps

    at my door, starving
  for a drink. I tell it to stop for a moment
and think.

    The branches of a tree
  on a day in winter crack in the wind's
pent-up anger.

    This broken doll I made whole
  for you is all I need to feed
my muse.

24

I shop for Today.
        It's bric-a-brac.
I bet on the Past.
It's
last on the track.
    I map the Future, falling like snow.
I stop by the Present,
but it's all show.

So then
I call on
        the never-say-die
where leaves trap the sun
even as it flies,
    where something wild
like the seed
of a carrot
cries underground, *I just can't bear it!*
        Pops out its leaves
and shoots the breeze,
no longer smothered, no longer
squeezed.

Where a man with a hoe
   (not yours, not mine)
takes care of our garden
all the time,
    and everything we'll ever know
takes off its shoes, wiggles its toes,
     and swims naked
in a long cool river,
   where it slowly sheds
twenty-four fevers,
       while
a tingle of trees, a long way off,
grows ordered and still. Holds
  the sky aloft.

25

      Can you draw the sap
from a wild cherry tree?
Can you teach the sparrow not to fly free?
      Can the clouds in the sky become
river sand?
Does the birch tree crawl
when it's just learned to stand?

      Does the silence of flowers
mean they can't talk?
          Does a blackboard of stars
mean they're just chalk?   No (and don't sulk)

      So the fact that you're gone, doesn't mean
you're not here.
Yet how I miss you!
   Though I don't shed a tear.

      Does the door that is flat
ever rise to the ceiling?
   The door you slam, open on hinges?
Does the window of your eye
   look out and in?
Are the two worlds it sees somehow blood kin?

When you're ready
to love, are you ready to fight?
Is spirit real? Is the sun full of light?   Yes (that's right)

So the fact that you're here, doesn't mean
you're not gone.
God, how I miss you! Can right go so wrong?

            But bad or good, old or young,
              come live with me all our lives long.
Or I'll sing you forever this wretched song.

26

Vision comes only when I'm blind.
    Then I touch each thing to see if it's mine.
I smell the roses before they bloom.
I chew its wisdom, then swallow my food.
  I hear water babies in the creek
    splash when they play, rock in their sleep.
I listen to pollen, kneaded full-grown
    to honey purling in waxen combs.

I hear music shaped just for my ears,
    enclosing the far in the very near. I follow
  the light by the warmth on my skin. To the edge
of the sunset I take it in. Twilight has footsteps
  that follow me home. Night has a face I mold with
    my thumb. Bed is a feather that teases the air.
Sleep is a silence that drifts without care
    on dreams

that move from earth to attic, from Medusa's stone face
    to Mary's—ecstatic. Though I am blind,
  still I can see how the madness of murder
turns to the sweet sun-ripened spirit, heady as wine.
   I breathe a perfume made just in time.
   I touch all the hills I used to know.
Black elephants I called them.
    Now they are snow.

Llewellyn McKernan is a poet, children's book writer, and teacher who has lived and worked in Huntington, WV, for over thirty years. She has a Master's Degree in Creative Writing from Brown University and a Master's in English from the University of Arkansas.

She has been an adjunct English professor at St. Mary's College, the University of Arkansas, and Marshall University. Among the eleven writing grants she has received are ones from the American Association of University Women, the West Virginia Commission on the Arts, and the West Virginia Humanities Council. Her work has won ninety-six prizes, awards, and honors in state, regional, and national contests. It has also appeared in forty-three anthologies and in such journals as *The Kenyon Review, Appalachian Journal, Southern Poetry Review, Antietam Review, Appalachian Heritage, Now & Then,* and others.

Five of her poetry books for adults have been published: *Short and Simple Annals, Many Waters, Llewellyn McKernan's Greatest Hits, Pencil Memory,* and *The Sound of One Tree Falling.* Four poetry books for children have also been published: *More Songs of Gladness, Bird Alphabet, This Is The Day,* and *This Is The Night.* Almost all these achievements occurred while she was living in West Virginia, where she still lives with her husband on a rural route. "If home is where the heart is," she says, "writing poetry is always home to me, and I've written more poems in West Virginia than anywhere else on earth."

www.ingramcontent.com/pod-product-compliance
Lightning Source LLC
LaVergne TN
LVHW041554070426
835507LV00011B/1085